DEDICATION

For my mother and father who, through their own marriage, have shown me that love requires plenty of hard work—but that the reward is a beautiful adventure full of laughter, sweetness, and precious memories. I love you both.

INTRODUCTION

Every day offers a new opportunity to share your love for that special someone! In the juggle of work, home, and social responsibilities, you can forget to infuse demonstrations of love into your life with your partner. Luckily, showing your love doesn't have to mean huge, sweeping gestures (although those can be fabulous too). Whether it's buying a bouquet of roses or making their favorite cup of coffee, your actions show that you care. *Simple Acts of Love* shares easy, everyday ways to show your partner how much you love them, including:

- Touring locations that are meaningful to you both
- Keeping their favorite snack on hand
- Slipping a love note into their suitcase before a trip
- Truly listening when they are speaking to you

SIMPLE ACTS OF LOVE

500 Little Ways to Make a BIG Difference in Your Relationship

MARIA DEL RUSSO

ADAMS MEDIA
NEW YORK AMSTERDAM/ANTWERP LONDON TORONTO
SYDNEY/MELBOURNE NEW DELHI

Adams Media
An Imprint of Simon & Schuster, LLC
100 Technology Center Drive
Stoughton, MA 02072

This Adams Media trade paperback edition December 2025

ADAMS MEDIA and colophon are registered trademarks of Simon & Schuster, LLC.

Interior design by Julia Jacintho
Interior images © 123RF/Ivan Feoktistov, Rondale

Manufactured in the United States of America

2 2025

ISBN 978-1-5072-2643-8
ISBN 978-1-5072-1040-6 (ebook)

- Cleaning up after yourself in a shared bathroom
- Getting to know their close friends
- Delivering their favorite takeout to their office

And the more you show love to one another, the more love you'll cultivate. Once you start being more mindful of showing your love, you'll be amazed by how quickly it becomes second nature. You'll also find that when you implement acts of love throughout your daily life with your partner, you'll inspire them to do the same. So, whether you're hoping to maintain the passion or reignite the spark; whether you've been together for five weeks, five months, or five years—flip through the pages ahead for simple ways to bring you and your partner closer together!

Start your morning with a ***kiss***—even if you went to bed angry, or you haven't brushed your teeth yet. You subconsciously make a choice every day to be with the person sleeping next to you. Planting one on their lips first thing each morning shows your partner that, once again, you're choosing them and the love you two share.

Send them flowers for no reason. Flowers are wonderful gifts for special occasions, but flowers for no reason? Magic. Bonus points if you send a bouquet to their office. Who doesn't love to show off the ***beautiful blooms*** their partner sent them to admiring coworkers?

If your partner has a good relationship with their parents, strive to maintain a relationship with them too. You don't necessarily have to pick up the phone and chat with them for hours, but something as simple as sending a text message to check in or wish them a ***happy birthday*** will go a long way in showing your partner that their family means a lot to you too.

If you wake up first, fix their ***coffee or tea*** the way they like it and bring it back to bed with you. There's something sweet—and sexy—about starting the day in bed together with a cup of your favorite morning beverage.

Every once in a while, do a small task that your partner is normally in charge of. This could be emptying the dishwasher, feeding the pets, or picking up the wine on your way to a dinner party. This seemingly insignificant act goes a long way in showing your partner that you recognize and ***appreciate*** the little things they do for your relationship.

IF THEY HAVE A FAVORITE *snack*, MAKE SURE TO KEEP IT AROUND FOR THEM TO ENJOY—ESPECIALLY WHILE TRAVELING TOGETHER.

Include them in your decisions. These decisions could be as small as asking them what book to read next, or as big as choosing to change jobs. Asking their *opinion* shows your partner that their input matters to you.

The next time they ask you where you want to go out to eat, ***tell them***. You may think that saying "wherever you want to go" is considerate because you're putting the decision in their hands. But consider the possibility that they may not want to make the decision alone, or that they may find joy in letting you choose.

Pay attention when they mention something they want but can't (or won't) spend the money on themselves, and keep a *running list* in your phone. When a special occasion comes around, you'll know exactly what to get them. The gift will be twice as meaningful, too, because it shows that you listen.

Write them a little *love note* and slip it into their suitcase before they go on a trip. The note can be as short and sweet or as long and involved as you want. The fact that you took the time to write it will make your partner smile and feel loved.

TALK YOUR PARTNER UP A LITTLE WHEN YOU'RE AMONG FRIENDS OR FAMILY MEMBERS. THIS DOESN'T MEAN YOU HAVE TO BRAG FOR AN HOUR ABOUT HOW INCREDIBLE THEY ARE, BUT IF THEY HAVE ACCOMPLISHED SOMETHING AT WORK OR HAVE COMPLETED A PERSONAL GOAL, DO A LITTLE GLOATING FOR THEM. YOUR PARTNER MIGHT BLUSH A BIT, BUT KNOWING THAT YOU'RE *proud* OF THEM IS AN UNBEATABLE FEELING.

Do something they *really* don't want to do, like booking the flights for your next trip together or cleaning out the cat's litter box. Doing so will not only show your partner that you care; it will also likely ***inspire*** them to pick up the slack somewhere down the line when it comes to something *you* don't want to do.

The next time you're out in public together, plant a little ***kiss*** on the nape of their neck. It's a subtle yet sexy gesture that clearly demonstrates that your partner is the person you're there with. Plus, this saucy action holds plenty of promise about what's to come when you return home together.

Plan a ***unique*** date night that's far outside the realm of what you two usually do together. A museum visit, cooking class, brewery tour, or comedy show are all easy ways to shake up your usual date routine, ensuring that things never feel too monotonous for you or your partner.

Clean your hair out of the bathroom. Seriously. Whether it's long strands in the bathtub drain or whiskers on the sink, taking five seconds to ensure there's no errant hairs around will show your partner that you ***respect*** your shared space. Plus, it makes cleaning *so* much easier for both of you.

If they tend to be the one in charge of dinner, put on your apron and whip them up their *favorite meal* one night. It shows how well you know their preferences, plus they will likely be *insanely* happy to take a night off from cooking.

Initiate sex, especially if your partner is typically the one to take the lead. Everyone likes to feel desired, so taking the reins in physical *intimacy* will show your partner how much they turn you on. And if they tend to be the more dominating one in bed, feel free to let them lead once things have heated up. However, a little role reversal can keep things fresh and show your partner that you're open to experimenting—which may be the ultimate turn-on for them.

Be ***vulnerable*** with them. Don't be afraid to tear up during a sad movie or share why you're feeling anxious on a particular day. The moments when you open up to your partner strengthen your bond. They may love how strong you are, but demonstrating your softer side shows that you want them to see every part of you.

Participate in activities they like—even if you dislike them. Waking up early to hit the farmers' market on a Saturday morning may sound terrible to you, or you may not understand your partner's need to sit in a bar and watch football for hours on end, but showing up for them in these moments demonstrates that you care about what makes them ***happy***. There is a caveat, however: if you're going to participate, you should try to *joyfully* participate—no sitting in the corner and sulking!

Truly *listen* when they talk to you. Put your phone down. Turn your eyes away from your computer. Mute the television. What may seem like idle chitchat to you may be important to your partner, so make sure your attention is completely on them. You may be surprised by what you learn.

Compliment them on the small things. If you think they look particularly handsome in a specific shirt, tell them. If you like the color of the dress they're wearing, let them know. Little compliments add up over time and show that you appreciate your partner.

GIVE THEM LITTLE KISSES AND *hugs* THROUGHOUT THE DAY. NO REASON NEEDED, OTHER THAN THE FACT THAT YOU LOVE THEM.

DON'T FORGET TO *flirt*—
EVEN IF YOU'VE BEEN TOGETHER FOR DECADES. FLIRTING IS WHAT HELPS KEEP THAT LOVE SPARK ALIVE, AND IT ADDS A LITTLE SEXINESS TO THE RELATIONSHIP WHEN THINGS MAY HAVE FALLEN INTO A COMFORTABLE RHYTHM.

Check in with your relationship. This doesn't necessarily mean that you need to make an appointment with a couples' therapist, but it does mean that you should ask your partner how they are feeling about things from time to time. *Open communication* is the hallmark of a solid relationship, and regular check-ins ensure the wheels are well greased.

GIVE THEM A *foot rub*, ESPECIALLY IF THEIR JOB REQUIRES THAT THEY ARE ON THEIR FEET FOR HOURS AT A TIME.

If they're training for a marathon, offer to go running with them. Sure, you can be *supportive* from the sidelines, but getting involved with their training shows that you two are a team—and that is priceless.

Thank them when they do something small for you or your relationship, like bringing you a glass of water or taking out the trash. These actions may seem insignificant, but they are an important part of your bond, and your ***acknowledgment*** will go a long way.

Surprise them at their office with an offer to take them out to lunch. Everyone loves a little midday break, and treating them to a ***meal*** out of the office is a sweet gesture. Not enough time to go to a restaurant? Bring some sandwiches to share at a nearby park.

If they're out without you, call the bar or restaurant they are at and order a ***round of drinks*** or an appetizer for their table. It shows your partner that you care about them having a good time—even when you aren't with them.

Give them the *space* to enjoy things on their own. Sure, the two of you might have many shared interests, but giving your partner time to do things solo is a very healthy indicator that you're secure in your relationship—and that is a turn-on.

Turn in early and order a *pizza*. Who doesn't love a little dining à la mattress—crumbs be damned!

Offer to help members of their *family* without being asked. Connect their younger sibling to a friend who can help them get a job, move a couch out of their mother's basement, or help clean out their grandparents' garage. Stepping up for their family without being asked shows your partner that these people are just as important to you as your own immediate family, and that is priceless.

Teach them about something you love, whether it's your favorite television show or a hobby you've enjoyed since you were young. They may not become a fan like you, but it will help them to understand the things that make you happy.

GREET THEM WARMLY WHEN THEY COME ***home***. WRAP YOUR ARMS AROUND THEM, PULL THEM IN, AND GIVE THEM A KISS.

Send them things that remind you of them when you're apart. It could be a funny note about an ***inside joke*** or a photo of their favorite flower—anything that makes you think of them. Sending a sweet text or email will let them know they're never far from your mind.

The next time they're flying in from out of town, pick them up from the ***airport***. Not only will it win some major points in the love department, but you'll be able to have one of those airport reunions you usually only see in movies!

Don't underestimate the effect of a little gift, especially on a day when your partner doesn't expect it. A little trinket that has a ***deeper meaning*** can demonstrate your love more than a big-ticket item.

Go old-school and make them a ***playlist***. Use your music-streaming service to create a mix tailored to their tastes, and then send it their way via email to listen to while they work. Talk about an instant mood booster!

READ TO THEM IN BED. IT CAN BE A *book* YOU ENJOY, AN INTERESTING ARTICLE YOU READ EARLIER THAT DAY, OR A SERIES OF SOCIAL MEDIA POSTS THAT MADE YOU LAUGH. THE SIMPLE ACT OF SHARING SOMETHING TOGETHER THAT ISN'T A TELEVISION SHOW BEFORE YOU BOTH TURN IN FOR THE NIGHT CAN MAKE YOU BOTH FEEL CLOSER.

Plan a long ***trip*** together. Maybe it's backpacking through Europe or spending three weeks in Japan. Short trips are always fun, but planning something longer shows your partner you love them enough to spend an extended period of time with them.

Don't complain about their family members or friends, even when *they* are complaining about them. ***Respect*** their relationships enough to recognize when your partner is just having a rough time and needs to vent, and don't join in on the piling on.

Perform *favors* without expecting something in return, like picking up the milk on your way home from work or folding the laundry.

Work toward a common *goal*. Whether it's saving money for a trip, training for a race, or repainting the kitchen, working toward something together shows that you are a team.

Create a little *ritual* together and stick to it. It could be an after-dinner walk, a Sunday bike ride, or an episode of your favorite show every Wednesday night. Making regular time for your partner proves they are a major part of your life—and someone you plan to have around for a while.

Compromise ON THE BIG *AND* LITTLE THINGS.

Listen without trying to fix their problems. People are often so quick to try to offer advice in order to make their partner feel better, but sometimes all that person wants is someone to vent to. Be that ***listening ear***.

If you catch their eye from across a social event, give them a little ***wink***. It will instantly connect you, no matter how far apart you are.

Ask them how they're doing—not just to make conversation. Ask them how they're feeling about things like work, family, and their friends. Then, truly listen. It can be hard for some people to express their feelings, but sometimes all you've got to do is *ask*.

Hang out with their *friends*. Nothing says "I love you" like showing your partner that the people in their life are important to you too.

Don't sweat the small stuff. Everyone is forgetful from time to time, or experiences a case of butterfingers that causes something to break, or says something they don't mean. Let the *little things* roll off your back.

Surprise them with an extra-special ***date night***. Get all dressed up and go out for a fancy dinner or book a night at a swanky hotel. There's something sexy about room service.

Be aware when they might need an extra ***confidence*** boost. If they're facing a big presentation, planning to ask for a raise, or struggling to stay motivated in their workout, letting them know how amazing they are can be just what they need to push forward.

When fighting, be *mindful* to not raise your voice. Yelling never helps an argument in a healthy way and often just leads to an escalation. Instead, aim to calmly discuss the things that are bothering you in a way that is respectful and open-minded.

Make sure you're *fairly* splitting the expenses for things you share. If you both drink milk, eat cereal, or drive the car, divide those expenses. This could mean a 50/50 split or a slightly different division of costs if you have found (perhaps based on salaries or other circumstances) that works best for you both.

Look at a situation from their point of view. You may never agree on a subject, but the fact that you went that extra mile to try to understand their *perspective* shows that you appreciate their thoughts and feelings.

HOLD *hands* WHEN YOU WALK DOWN THE STREET. IT'S A SIMPLE GESTURE THAT SIGNIFIES THAT YOU AND YOUR PARTNER HAVE CHOSEN TO WALK THROUGH LIFE TOGETHER.

GIVE THEM A *massage*—WITHOUT EXPECTING ONE IN RETURN.

Be their shoulder to cry on when they need it. A good cry can help a bad situation, and having someone there to ***hold*** you and tell you it will be okay can make things feel so much better.

Have a ***lazy night*** in together. Order some pizza, sit on the couch, and watch your favorite television show. A night out can be fabulous, but not having to put real pants on is also a luxury.

Try something ***new*** together.
Take a cooking class, learn a new language, or taste a dish neither of you has had before. Shared experiences are the bedrock of a strong relationship, and trying something new is always fun.

Celebrate the things that make you two different. Exploring the complexities of a partner, and realizing how you differ, is an adventure in and of itself. And these differences are often how you complement each other! When you discover one of these differences, make a point to talk about it in a positive way.

Make them a ***handmade*** card, whether for a special occasion or just because. Make sure to write something sweet inside—canned sentiments are for commercial greeting cards.

Acknowledge the little ***skills*** that others may not recognize. Being intimate with someone means you know how well they make pie crust or how good they are at mediating an argument. Make sure to point these things out to your partner, because others may not.

Create a sweet ***nickname*** for them—that they're comfortable with, of course. Make sure it's something kind and not childish or insulting.

Create a ***photo album*** of all of the trips you've been on together. It may be cheesy and a bit old-school, but completing this project together will remind you both of the fun times you've had, with the added bonus of a special keepsake you can flip through at any time.

Hopeless in the kitchen? You can still "make" your partner a delicious meal. Pick up their favorite kind of ***takeout*** on the way home from work. And instead of eating it out of the plastic containers, plate the food like you would a home-cooked meal. Your partner will appreciate the effort, and it will jazz up your typical takeout dinner.

Split the family ***holidays*** in a way that makes sense for both of you. Spending time with their relatives during special occasions is tantamount to showing your love for your partner.

Write a ***vow***. Vows aren't just for weddings—nor do they need to be a pledge that you will be with that person until death do you part. A vow can be a promise of anything, from supporting your partner in good and bad times, to always making them laugh. Sharing a vow is a simple yet big way to show your love—plus, because it is written down, you can give it to them to keep.

Bring their ***parents*** something when you visit. It can be as simple as flowers, as thoughtful as a photo of you and your partner, or as lavish as an expensive bottle of wine. It's the thought that truly counts, and it shows your partner that their parents are important to you too.

IF THEY ASK YOU TO DO SOMETHING, DO IT *immediately*. DON'T PUT IT OFF UNTIL YOU FORGET AND THEY HAVE TO ASK AGAIN AND AGAIN.

Know what fights are ***worth it***. Not everything needs to be turned into some huge drama, and walking away shows that you know when to fight for your love and when to let things go.

Gift them a book that means something to you and highlight your ***favorite passages***. This small act gives your partner a look into a part of your life that's typically kept just for you, building the intimacy between you. Plus, sometimes your favorite writers can be better at expressing your thoughts or feelings than you are.

TELL THEM THAT THEY'RE ***right*** WHEN THEY ARE.

Let them take control of decisions that are important to them—especially if those decisions don't mean as much to you. Let them pick out the comforter in your bedroom or choose where you two go for dinner. It lets them know that you *trust* them to pick something you'll both enjoy.

When you're walking hand-in-hand, give their hand a little *squeeze*. It's a simple gesture that helps you feel even more connected.

Never underestimate the power of a ***head rub***—especially after sex.

If you wake up in the middle of the night and realize that their *covers* are mussed, fix them and tuck your partner back in.

Help them see their *potential*, especially when they can't see it themselves. This could mean reading and editing a story they're working on or listening to a song they've recorded. Cheering them on while they're attempting to accomplish something shows that you care about their success and that you believe in them.

Match their *enthusiasm* level. If they're excited about something, try to get excited about it too. If you couldn't care less about the thing, then find excitement in your partner's mood boost.

Turn your date night into a date *weekend* with a spur-of-the-moment trip somewhere. A bed and breakfast, mountain lodge, or beach cabin are all fun locations to ***mix things up***.

Sacrifice ***personal time*** in order to spend more time with them. This could mean skipping watching a baseball game or putting off finishing a book you were planning to get through. Putting the time you spend together above time you spend alone occasionally is a great way to show your partner how important they are to you.

Help them out—especially if it's with something you're great at but they struggle with. If they're hopeless at caulking a tub, give them a hand. If they can't cook duck to save their life, be their sous chef.

GIVE THEM A PASSIONATE KISS, ESPECIALLY IF THEY AREN'T EXPECTING IT. IT'S INCREDIBLE HOW QUICKLY THIS SMALL ROMANTIC ACT CAN BRING BACK THE *sparks*.

Cry in front of them. Your partner will relish the opportunity to comfort you when you need it. Trust them enough to show your *vulnerability*.

Make the bed. It's a quick and easy way to show that you care about your *shared space*.

SEND GOOD-MORNING AND GOOD-NIGHT *texts* IF YOU AREN'T LIVING TOGETHER.

Give them props when they accomplish a task that you know was challenging for them. Recognizing your partner's ***hard work*** and applauding them for a job well done is sure to make them swoon.

Send them a "thinking of you" text when they cross your ***mind*** during the day. It's a simple gesture that has quite an impact.

Talk about how you're feeling in the relationship. It can be scary, but ***sharing*** your fears or your hopes for a shared future shows your partner how much you trust them, which is the cornerstone of any strong relationship.

If they have a particular fantasy that you haven't tried out yet (and that you're comfortable with), spring it on them in the bedroom without warning. It's a sexy way to show them that you listen to them—and that you're interested in their *pleasure*.

Do something together that reminds you of your *childhood*. Build a pillow fort or blow bubbles. It's easy to be serious, but it takes true intimacy to be silly with one another.

Explore your ***kinky*** side together with a trip to an adult toy store. Even if you don't buy anything, it could spark a conversation about what you'd both like to try in bed.

Have a movie marathon night. You can try picking ***movies*** neither of you has seen before to make it extra special.

CALL AHEAD TO COVER THE EXPENSE BEFORE THEY ARRIVE TO AN APPOINTMENT SUCH AS A HAIRCUT OR MANICURE. YOU CAN BET THAT YOUR PARTNER'S FACE WILL *light up* WHEN THEY GO TO THE REGISTER TO PAY AND HEAR THAT YOU'VE HANDLED IT.

Help them *reconnect* with someone important in their life, be it a friend or a family member. This could take different forms, from helping them draft an email, to listening when they talk about their feelings for that person. Helping repair or fortify those connections is a great way to show your partner that you're on their team.

If you're out at a party together, pull them in close and *whisper* that you can't wait to have them alone later. It's incredibly sexy—and sets a romantic mood for the rest of the night.

PICK UP THE *latest issue* OF THEIR FAVORITE MAGAZINE. OR, BETTER YET, BUY THEM A SUBSCRIPTION AS A SURPRISE.

Pull them in for a *slow dance*—whether it's at a wedding or in the middle of your kitchen while you're cooking dinner. You don't need any music playing to enjoy this intimate moment.

Show a little social media PDA (as long as they're comfortable with it). Showing them off on social media demonstrates to the world how important your partner is to you. Keep in mind there are ***tasteful*** ways to do this that won't make other people's stomachs turn.

Take the time to ***understand*** their feelings. Don't just brush them off. Allow your partner the time and space to explain themselves, and accept the fact that this is the way they're feeling—whether you agree with those emotions or not.

LEARN TO CONFRONT WITHOUT CRITICIZING. IT'S EASIER FOR YOU AND YOUR PARTNER TO FIND *common ground* WHEN YOU AREN'T FLINGING INSULTS AT ONE ANOTHER.

Be on *time*. "I'm always late" isn't a good excuse. Leave yourself plenty of time to be there for your partner at the time you agreed to. It's the ultimate sign of respect.

Don't talk poorly about your past relationships. You may feel that speaking ill about former partners or relationships will help your current partner recognize how special they are, but this is a common misconception. You show respect for your partner by showing *respect* for the people you shared a past with. When in doubt, don't bring them up.

Cuddle WITH THEM WHENEVER POSSIBLE.

Don't have important conversations over text messaging. Even if they're the one trying to discuss details or start an argument, let them know that you'd rather talk about it in person—and then have that conversation when the time comes. It's easy for emotions and intentions to be misinterpreted over text messages, and for one or both people to feel as though what they are saying isn't being properly acknowledged or even noticed. When you're sitting with your partner, you're acting as a unit, and it's easier to find a satisfying ***resolution*** to a problem.

Throw them a ***surprise party***. A birthday is the obvious occasion, but you can do it just for fun too. Extra points if you get their friends involved in the ruse.

Bake their ***favorite dessert***. If they don't love sweets, pick them up their favorite snack.

If you wake up before them, be as quiet as possible as you leave the room. Having a few extra minutes of uninterrupted ***sleep*** is absolutely blissful.

Tell them how much they mean to you. It's easy to forget to say these things to one another. Explaining how much you love seeing them in the morning, or how you can't wait to get ***home*** to them at night, can be more meaningful than your usual "I love you."

Take care of the *morning chores* so they can sleep in. Take the dog for a walk, take the trash out, fold the laundry, or whatever else might have kept them from getting those extra zzz's.

Take *care* of them when they're sick.
It's miserable being alone when you aren't feeling well, so when you are there to ensure that they're drinking enough water or that they have enough blankets, it will make a huge difference for them. Just don't complain about possibly getting sick yourself: it will only make your partner feel worse.

If they're hungover, bring them their favorite hangover *cure*. Or simply leave them alone if that's what they want.

If one of you isn't a big fan of ***cuddling***, figure out another way to be close that works for both of you.

Go to a movie they want to see but you have no interest in. Sure, you may not care about the latest rom-com, but ***spending time*** on the things your partner enjoys shows how much they mean to you.

Pick up something you know they always need more of, like their favorite pens or the brand of toothpaste they prefer. It's always good to have an extra supply of the thing you use regularly, and this simple act shows your partner that you take notice of those ***little details***.

Instead of rushing home after a dinner out, go for a ***leisurely*** walk or drive. Enjoy the in-between times that you spend together just as much as those planned events.

ON A COLD OR SNOWY DAY, BRING YOUR PARTNER A HOT CHOCOLATE—EITHER HOMEMADE OR FROM YOUR LOCAL COFFEE SHOP. IT'S A SWEET AND *nostalgic* WAY FOR THEM TO WARM UP. ADD MARSHMALLOWS OR WHIPPED CREAM FOR AN EXTRA-SPECIAL TOUCH.

If you know they love you in a certain outfit, wear it for them on any old day. Not only will your partner love the fact that you've dressed for them; *you* may also find it incredibly ***sexy*** to know your partner is turned on by the way you look.

Ask for their ***advice***. The subject doesn't matter: it could be as small as which brand of oat milk to buy, or as large as whether or not to switch careers. Taking your partner's thoughts into consideration shows how much you value their opinion.

Take the time to learn their friends' ***names***. Nothing says "I care about you" more than referring to their friend as "Allison" and not "the one who works in finance."

Follow up on things they talked about earlier, like an argument they had at work or a class they were hoping to take. See how they're feeling about it now, and ask if there is anything you can do to help things progress.

Run them a ***bath***. Fill it with fancy extras, like bath salts, bubbles, and essential oils. Light a few candles, play some soothing music, and give them the space to just enjoy themselves.

Gift them a picture of the two of you. It can be a posed portrait of an event where you were both looking your best or a *candid* taken somewhere meaningful for you.

Don't be afraid to fight when necessary. Arguments happen—especially when both partners are passionate about something. A little disagreement can even be *healthy*: research shows that these tussles can signal the need for change in both parties, which helps you and your partner grow together in the partnership and as individuals.

Set a monthly date night. *Routine* may not seem all that romantic, but in cases like this, it shows that you care enough to carve time with them into your regular schedule.

Tell them how much you appreciate the ***little ways*** in which they make your life easier, like how they always remember to pick up milk from the grocery store or are always unloading the dishwasher. These acts rarely get recognition, so letting your partner know that you are appreciative will make them happier than you know.

Come to a ***compromise*** with communication preferences. If they like to text throughout the day, while you prefer to keep the messages focused on major plans or important information, find a middle ground. Happy relationships are ones in which both partners' needs are being met, so figure out a way to make you both satisfied.

Set the table before dinner, especially if they're the one making the meal. You can make it extra special with the "good china" and some candles if you're feeling ***fancy***.

When watching a movie or TV show on the couch, move in close to them. *Physical* closeness is just as important as emotional closeness.

RUN YOUR FINGERS THROUGH THEIR *hair* AS YOU'RE KISSING. IT'S SEXY—AND FEELS AMAZING.

Take a bath together. Fill it up with bubbles and sweet-smelling oils. Light some *candles*, wash each other's hair, and see where the night takes you.

If you live separately, make sure their *favorite wine* or beer is in your fridge. It shows that you consider their happiness when stocking your home.

Kiss them on the *forehead*. It's a sweet move that can be more intimate than a smooch on the lips.

Remember their preferences for things like type of milk, toasted or untoasted bagel, and side of the bed they like to sleep on. It's a simple way to show you care.

CRY TOGETHER. ONE OF YOU DOESN'T ALWAYS HAVE TO BE STRONG FOR THE OTHER. THERE IS TRUE INTIMACY IN SHARED *emotion*.

Use the words *us* and *we* in conversation as much as you can. It helps remind your partner that you are a ***unit***. There's also something special about overhearing yourself referred to as part of the "we" in a conversation your partner is having with others.

If they have a car, clean it out or take it for an oil change. No one loves these ***tasks***, so having someone help out is extra special.

Send a sexy, ***flirty*** text message when they're least expecting it. It doesn't have to be that raunchy (although those are fun too), but something simmering and sensual to get you both in the mood for later.

Try to schedule your ***bedtimes*** so they're at the same time. No one likes to fall asleep alone, and being able to curl up next to someone you love is a great feeling.

Open the door for them, whether it's the car door or the door to a restaurant.

Put the toilet ***seat*** down—or put it up, depending on how your partner uses it.

Come up with a creative way to tell each other that you love one another: a wink, nod, or hand gesture any way to ***communicate*** "I love you" in public without saying it out loud.

CREATE A SAFE WORD FOR HEATED ARGUMENTS. WHEN THINGS ARE HEADED TOWARD A BREAKING POINT, IMPLEMENT THE SAFE WORD AND TAKE FIVE MINUTES FOR EACH OF YOU TO COOL OFF. ONCE YOU ARE MORE *calm*, YOU CAN TALK ABOUT WHAT HAPPENED.

Go to a museum together. Take the time to walk around and *discuss* what you like about each piece, and be sure to hold hands as you walk.

If they suffer from a chronic ailment, like migraines or back pain, create a *first aid kit* for them with all the things that tend to make them feel better. Make sure it's always well stocked.

Don't have the funds to go away for vacation? Try a ***staycation*** together. Book a room at a nearby hotel for an evening in town. Even though you are close to home, spending the night in a different bed and waking up to a different view in the morning will breathe new life into your bond.

Don't just roll over and fall asleep after having sex. Lie together for a while. You don't have to talk: just looking at one another and being in each other's company is enough to bring your intimacy to an even ***deeper*** level.

Look into one another's ***eyes*** when you're speaking—or when you're just sitting together quietly. Love shows through the eyes.

Give them a *day off*. Run their errands, cook their meals, and handle their responsibilities (within reason). Encourage them to kick their feet up or do an activity they're usually too busy to enjoy.

Keep track of those smaller anniversaries (your first kiss, the day you moved in together) in your phone so you'll *remember* them on the day. On that day, mention it to your partner and enjoy the happy trip down memory lane together.

Ask how you can help them. Not everyone thinks to ask when they could use some *assistance*, and being able to help your partner in even a small way will feel great for you both.

Is their favorite band coming to town (or a town nearby)? Pick up tickets as a *surprise*.

If the weather report says it's going to rain, make sure they have an ***umbrella***. This is especially good if your partner tends to be forgetful.

SUGGEST A BOOK FOR YOU TWO TO *read together*—LIKE A COUPLE'S BOOK CLUB! WHEN YOU'RE BOTH FINISHED WITH THE BOOK, TAKE THE TIME TO DISCUSS WHAT YOU LIKED AND DIDN'T LIKE ABOUT IT. THEN, LET YOUR PARTNER CHOOSE THE NEXT BOOK YOU READ.

Pick up the ***check*** from time to time. During a meal out is a typical time to do this, but you can also cover their share during less obvious moments too. Get their coffee, buy them the pair of shoes they just tried on, or pay for their gas when you two are driving together.

Pack them lunch. It can be leftovers or a sandwich that you made from scratch. The fact that you took the time to make a ***yummy meal*** so they wouldn't have to worry about it later will speak volumes.

If you notice their hands get chapped in the winter, ***pick up*** some hand lotion. Stash it in their purse or work bag so they can use it when needed.

Help them get more ***organized***, especially if it's something they struggle with. Tackle their side of the closet, or help them put their glove compartment in order. They'll think of you every time things run smoothly in the future.

PULL THEM IN FOR A BIG ***hug***. KISSES ARE GREAT, BUT THERE'S SOMETHING EXTRA SPECIAL ABOUT A BIG BEAR HUG.

Stroke their hair when you're sitting next to them. It's a small, intimate gesture that shows your partner how ***comfortable*** you are with them.

Bring them *breakfast* in bed. It doesn't have to be anything gourmet: Cheerios seem extra special when presented in bed. Don't forget a serving tray and flower for an even sweeter touch.

Vary your lovemaking from time to time. Don't rely on the same three positions. Try something new. One night, it might be slow and sensual. Another, it might be quick and passionate. And if you want to find new positions to try, just look online. Variety is the *spice* of life, after all—especially when it comes to sex.

Take control of planning your night out, especially if your partner is usually the one to put things together. Planning takes more *effort* than you might expect, so it's a fantastic feeling to get the night off from the responsibility.

IF THEY'VE TAKEN THE TIME TO REALLY GET DRESSED UP, GIVE THEM AN EXTRA-SPECIAL *compliment*. EVERYONE LIKES TO KNOW WHEN THEIR EFFORT HAS BEEN NOTICED.

If it's going to be cold in the morning, put their robe and/or *slippers* somewhere they can grab them as soon as they slip out of bed. No one likes to get hit with a shock of cold air first thing, so it's a sweet way to show your partner that you've considered their comfort.

Fix their broken phone screen—especially if they've been putting it off because of the expense. It's a ***small investment*** in their comfort. Plus, there are ways they can pay you back that don't cost any money at all.

Don't use up all the hot water. Seriously. Everyone loves a ***hot shower***, but leave some for your partner too.

If they've lost something, help them ***find*** it. Crawl on your knees for the back piece of an earring, or call the bar to look for their lost wallet. Don't let them suffer through the anxiety alone.

If they have a *pet*, take care of it when they're out of town. Pet owners feel extremely attached to their four-legged friends, and knowing they are in safe hands is a huge relief. So take it for a walk, bring it to the vet if it seems ill or is injured, and send plenty of pictures to your partner!

Keep your phone in your bag or pocket during dinner. You don't need that picture of your meal. Instead, take the time to be fully *present* with your partner.

Be supportive of their big ideas.
They may seem completely outlandish to you, and your partner may recognize that too, but showing that you *support* them through whatever is important to them will mean everything to them.

Ask how they are *feeling* today. A regular check-in with your partner about where they are at emotionally not only shows that you care but also helps you figure out what their current needs may be.

Don't expect the worst. Your partner can sense when you're waiting for the other shoe to drop. Instead, give yourself over to the insecurities that are common in a relationship, and let your partner know that you're ***committed*** to riding the roller coaster with them.

Do something for the first time together. It can be as extravagant as bungee jumping or as simple as picking a new sushi roll to try at your favorite spot. These first times create special ***memories***.

Allow them to mess up without *comment*.
If your partner committed an "oops," they know it. Let them correct their mistake without pointing out what they did wrong or what they could have done better—unless they ask for feedback, of course.

Don't argue about money. Figure out each of your stress points and obstacles when it comes to finances and come up with ways to discuss money calmly and *constructively*.

Take them *shopping* if they're unhappy with their wardrobe. You can even pick out something together, and that garment will forever be extra special to you both.

Pull them onto the dance floor when you're at a wedding or party. Even if you can't ***dance*** to save your life, everyone loves a partner who isn't afraid to get down in public.

Fill up their car with gas.

Surprise them with a ***gift card*** to their favorite coffee shop.

Write them a little ***note*** on the bathroom mirror in the steam from your shower. Silly? Yes. But there's no way it won't make your partner smile.

IF THEY'VE BEEN OUT OF TOWN, MAKE SURE THEY'RE COMING HOME TO A *clean space*. VACUUM, WIPE DOWN ANY DUSTY SURFACES, AND MAKE SURE ALL THE DISHES ARE CLEAN. BETTER YET, CHANGE THE SHEETS: EVERYONE LOVES SLIPPING INTO A FRESHLY MADE BED AFTER A LONG JOURNEY.

Go *deep*. Have a long, meaningful conversation with your partner. It doesn't have to be about your feelings or your relationship: philosophical conversations have a way of drawing out the hidden parts of a person, which can create a deeper intimacy between you and your partner.

PULL YOUR PARTNER OUTSIDE FOR SOME *stargazing*.

Don't interrupt them. Allow them to *finish* their sentences without jumping in with a similar story or your opinion on their situation.

Apologize when you're wrong or when you've hurt them. "I'm sorry" can sometimes feel like the hardest words in the world to say. For that very reason, they're also two of the most *powerful* words you can speak to your partner.

Treat them the way you want to be treated. It's an old adage, but it's true! Don't compare them to others and always respect the fact that they are a ***unique*** individual. That is, of course, why you love them so much.

Tell them when you're ***proud*** of them. Knowing that a partner is in awe of you is an unmatched feeling.

WRITE THEM A *poem*—EVEN IF IT'S A HAIKU, AND EVEN IF YOU THINK YOU'RE TERRIBLE AT POETRY.

Order a pizza, and ask the pizza place to spell out "I Love You" in pepperoni on top. It's ***cheesy*** (in more ways than one) but sweet!

Whenever they do something you love, make a little ***note*** of it in a notebook. At the end of the year, give them the notebook, thanking them for such a special year.

Have a grown-up ***slumber party***. Go all out: play games, cuddle in front of the TV, and instigate a pillow fight.

Give their shoulder a little ***squeeze*** when they've done something that you find charming.

Do go to bed angry when the situation calls for it. An argument that seemed ***gigantic*** the night before can shrink to a speck by morning. After getting some sleep, you may realize that there was nothing to be angry about after all.

Start a ***hobby*** together. Pick up ice skating or start your own movie club. Shared experiences are the easiest way to feel closer to your partner!

Order ***balloons*** delivered to their office. This is especially effective if they aren't fond of flowers—and who doesn't love balloons?

Take a ***class*** together. A cooking class is a typical choice, but it's not the only one. Try a wine tasting class or learn a foreign language. Having a "study buddy" can also be incredibly sexy.

LET THEM KNOW WHEN THEY HAVE SOMETHING IN THEIR TEETH OR WHEN THEIR BREATH SMELLS BAD. AWKWARD? MAYBE. APPRECIATED? *Always.*

If they don't want to come to an ***event*** with you, let them stay home. No one can be social *all* the time, after all.

If they love to read, make them a ***bookmark*** covered in little love notes or pictures of the two of you.

If you're apart for an extended period of time, have a standing ***video chat*** appointment. Texting and calling is great, but a little face-to-face time trumps all.

Have a quickie before heading out to a party or other event. You'll both enjoy walking around with a sexy little *secret* all night long.

Anticipate their needs. If they say they're coming down with a headache, pour them a glass of water and hand them some pain relievers. If it looks like it's going to snow, ensure that they have a hat or mittens when they leave.

Make an effort to avoid issues that are triggering for them. Bringing up a touchy topic may seem like a joke to you, but it can easily disrupt your partner's *mood* and even affect them long after the comment is made.

Tell them why they're special. People can't always see these things for themselves. Knowing that your partner sees and loves your little ***quirks*** is incredibly validating.

The next time you travel, suggest that you both keep a separate ***journal*** for the trip. When you get home, read one another's accounts of the day.

Take a few minutes after your alarm clock goes off to ***snuggle*** in bed before rushing off to work. Those few minutes spent together in the morning are special and can set the tone for the rest of your day.

FIX THEM A LITTLE *snack*, JUST BECAUSE.

Follow "I love you" with a reason why. Anyone can share their feelings, but backing it up with a ***reason*** makes the sentiment that much stronger.

Help them choose an ***outfit*** ahead of a big meeting. Knowing that you've had a hand in making sure they look their best will boost their confidence all day long.

If they have to wake up early one day, ***wake up*** with them. No one loves waking up early alone. Plus, you can fall right back asleep once they leave.

Plan ahead for the both of you. If they're going to have a long day, make sure there's something quick to put together for dinner later. It makes both of your lives easier in the long run.

Show up to the things that matter, even when they tell you that you don't have to. Some partners say no to ***support*** that they actually want or need. Knowing the difference shows that you know them.

If you're headed out of town, leave them little notes to ***find*** while you're gone. They can be in their work bag or in a bathroom drawer they use daily—anywhere you know your partner will come across them.

CELEBRATE THE LITTLE *milestones* IN YOUR RELATIONSHIP, LIKE THE FIRST TIME YOU EXCHANGED KEYS OR THE FIRST TIME YOU TRAVELED TOGETHER. THESE SMALL MOMENTS ARE JUST AS SPECIAL AS THE LARGER ONES, BUT THEY DON'T TEND TO GET THE SAME RECOGNITION. GIVING THEM THEIR PROPS SHOWS YOUR PARTNER THAT YOU CARE ABOUT *EVERY* PART OF YOUR RELATIONSHIP.

Give them specific ***compliments***. "Your eyes really pop in that dress" packs a much larger punch than "You look nice."

If you're ***crafty***, make them a handmade gift. A piece of furniture you built or a blanket you knitted can be more special than a store-bought gift.

If you know they're having a bad day, have a little something ***sweet*** waiting for them when they get home. It can be a bouquet of flowers, a glass of wine, or their favorite chocolates—anything that can turn their day around.

IF THERE'S ONLY ONE PHONE CHARGER AVAILABLE, LET THEM USE IT ***first***.

If you're out to dinner without them, bring them home a ***doggy bag***. The easiest way to a person's heart is through the stomach, after all!

If you bring them to a party where they don't know many people, make sure they're comfortable and taken care of. Don't leave them alone in a group of strangers: introduce them, keep them ***company***, and help them have the best time they can.

Keep a ***picture*** of them in your wallet.

Notice their stomach rumbling? Whip them up a ***healthy treat***. Everyone loves to indulge, but showing that you also care about your partner's health shows that you care about them.

Put away ***leftovers*** and other items after they've cooked.

Step in when they're too tired or overwhelmed to complete a task—even if it's something they've insisted they can finish solo. Sometimes people bite off more than they can chew. Stepping in (without gloating!) is both helpful and loving.

Give them an over-the-top ***welcome*** when they walk through the door. Show them how much you've missed them—even if they've only been gone for a short amount of time.

Send them a text detailing how excited you are to do "x" later. It can be as PG or X-rated as you'd like. Building desire and ***anticipation*** is a surefire way to show your partner how much you want them.

If you read an article you think they'd enjoy, send it their way. An ***informed*** couple is a happy couple, after all!

Let them pick the ***restaurant*** the next time you go out to eat.

Use a picture of them as your smartphone ***background***. Seeing themselves reflected in your everyday life will make them feel loved.

Take a *dance* class together, especially ahead of a big event where dancing is involved. Even if you never truly master the box step, just putting the time and effort into learning together is meaningful.

If you don't want to go to an event with them, but you know it is important to them, suck it up and go. If you need motivation, imagine the *smile* on your partner's face when you tell them that you'll be there for them.

SAY *hello* THE SECOND YOU WALK THROUGH THE DOOR. ACKNOWLEDGING THEM WHEN YOU ENTER A ROOM LETS THEM KNOW HOW SPECIAL THEY ARE TO YOU.

Crack the whip and be ***motivational*** when they need it. No matter how much a person wants to get something done, sometimes they need extra encouragement. Be their drill sergeant if they seem to be lagging—a kind sergeant, of course.

If they need to change their diet for any reason, be it an illness, pregnancy, or weight loss goal, be ***supportive*** by tweaking your diet too. No one enjoys eating healthy when their partner is indulging across the table.

If they use public transportation, make sure their subway or bus card balance is filled. There's nothing worse than having something avoidable impede your ability to get to work on time. Show them that you ***care*** about their ease of life.

Order their favorite ***drink*** for them the next time you're out to dinner. It's a small gesture that shows you remember the smallest things about them.

Split the financial burden of birth control. Whether it's condoms or pills, it's always helpful to know that both partners feel invested in one another's sexual ***health***.

If they ask you to run an errand, don't complain. This is an *opportunity* to lighten their load and show your love. They will deeply appreciate it.

If they've left dishes in the sink, *clean* them for them. It's a fantastic feeling to see that a task you thought you had yet to accomplish has already been taken care of.

Choose them over your friends from time to time. Sure, you love meeting your friends for your monthly poker game, but if that's also the evening of your partner's best friend's birthday party, or if you haven't had quality time with your partner in a while, *choose them*. There will always be next month.

Not sure what to wear for a special occasion? Pull out that shirt they like you in or apply that shade of lipstick they find ***sexiest*** on you. It's a simple way to make the event even more special.

Don't forget big ***events*** like anniversaries or birthdays. Write them in a calendar, be it digital or a physical copy kept in your kitchen.

Buy them lingerie or an equally sexy gift you can both ***enjoy*** in the bedroom.

PICK UP THE PHONE AND ***call*** THEM WHEN YOU'RE APART. IT'S MORE INTIMATE THAN TEXTING.

If they tend to get anxious, ask them how you can help mitigate the symptoms. And ask *after* a panic attack, not during. This way, you can be ***informed*** for the next time and not add to the stress of an attack that is already in progress.

SPEND TIME WITH THEIR FAMILY. SUGGESTING TIME TOGETHER WITH THE PEOPLE WHO ARE IMPORTANT TO THEM SHOWS YOUR PARTNER THAT YOU VALUE THEIR *connections* AS MUCH AS THEY DO.

Take their ***picture*** when they ask you to—without rolling your eyes. Everyone needs a social media spouse from time to time. Don't tease your partner about it.

Take care of yourself for them. Eat ***healthy*** and keep yourself looking fresh. It's hard to love someone who doesn't love themselves, so ensure you're keeping yourself in tip-top shape for your partner.

Develop a ***secret signal*** for when you want to leave an event early. It's fun *and* useful—plus, it gives you and your partner something special to share.

If they're a troubled sleeper, pick them up a sound machine or sweet-smelling *aromatherapy* oils. It shows that you're concerned with their health, and it will probably help your own snooze sessions too.

If they suggest something for you two to do together, don't brush it off—even if you have no interest in it. Understand that they want to include you in their world, so you should be *flexible* when it comes to their suggestions.

If they love wearing a piece of your clothing, and you can part with it, ***gift*** it to them.

If you're out in public and see something amiss about their outfit, fix it. Smooth out their collar, button a button that came undone, or tuck a stray hair behind their ear. It's a simple yet surprisingly sweet and sexy ***gesture*** that shows you care.

If they're going to be far away from their family for a big event, ask their family members to record ***video messages*** for them ahead of time. Edit the messages together into one video and play it for your partner on the big day.

Plan a ***picnic***. If there's a park or beach nearby, have it there. Or just set yourselves up in your backyard. Make some sandwiches, cut up some cheese, spread out a blanket, and enjoy yourselves.

Take them on a ***scavenger hunt*** of your relationship. Leave clues that lead to spots like where you had your first date, where you shared your first kiss, and your favorite coffee shop. Finish the hunt somewhere special—like a restaurant for a fancy date or back home for a sexy sleepover.

TALK ABOUT THE *future* WITH THEM. TALKING ABOUT CHILDREN AND MARRIAGE CAN BE SCARY, BUT IT SHOWS THAT YOU'VE THOUGHT OF THEM WHEN CONSIDERING YOUR FUTURE. AND SOMETIMES THE SCARIEST THINGS ARE THE ONES THAT BRING YOU CLOSER TOGETHER.

Ask them about their ***childhood***. Everyone loves to reminisce, and you may be surprised by what you find out.

Go for a long walk together. You may ***discover*** something with them that you would have never seen on your own.

Host a ***party*** together and invite a mix of your friends and theirs. This meshing of worlds under one roof can help you feel closer to each other. Plus, you can learn a lot about a person by how they interact with their pals.

Do something together that scares you. This could be as small as seeing a scary movie or as big as going skydiving. It's incredible how much a little ***adrenaline*** can bring two people together.

If you're packing their lunch for work, leave a little love ***note*** on the napkin you slip in their lunchbox.

Help their parent shop for the perfect holiday or birthday ***gift*** for them. It shows your partner that you care enough about their family to be involved in their decisions. Plus, it's an easy way to score points with your partner's parents, which is never a bad idea.

If they're a collector, gift them something to add to their *collection*. It may be something as small as a penny you found on the street, or as big as a first edition of a book.

If there is a picture that means a lot to them, get it professionally framed. It doesn't have to be a picture of the two of you—it could be a childhood *memory* or a photo of their beloved pet.

Don't be a nag. Instead of constantly asking them to do something they seem reluctant to do, try approaching the discussion from a *different angle*. Explain to them why you're asking and what the gesture would mean for you. And then figure out a way for that goal to be accomplished together.

DON'T BLAME THEM FOR YOUR MISTAKES—EVEN IN THE *heat* OF THE MOMENT.

Know when to stop joking around. There's a time for teasing, but if there's a *joke* that seems to rub your partner the wrong way, let it go.

Know how to be *honest* while also being kind. Everyone wants their partner to be open and honest with them. But there is a polite way to do it...and a mean way to do it. Being a good partner means knowing how to give criticism kindly.

Gift them the tools to see their *dreams* through. If they want to write a series of novels, buy them a notebook. If they want to travel to a foreign country, make sure your passports are up-to-date.

If they have a hobby, buy them something to go along with it. If they knit, buy them special yarn. If they collect records, get them a vintage vinyl. Anything that shows you care about their ***hobbies*** will mean the world to them.

Make their ***birthday*** special for them, regardless of your own thoughts about birthdays. Ask yourself what they would enjoy in a birthday—it may not be the typical party or cake. It's one day out of the year, but if it's special, they'll remember it forever.

APPRECIATE THEIR *advice*, WHETHER YOU'VE ASKED FOR IT OR NOT. WHETHER YOU USE OR EVEN CONSIDER IT, LET THEM KNOW THAT YOU HAVE ACKNOWLEDGED THEIR INPUT.

Get their favorite *lunch* delivered to their office. This is especially useful if you're not a good cook yourself.

SURPRISE THEM WITH FRESHLY BAKED *cookies* WHEN THEY WALK THROUGH THE DOOR.

If you're headed out of town, leave them a little care package to find and enjoy while you're away. It can be filled with snacks, tools for *pampering*, or a new book for them to read. Whatever it is, make sure it's something you know they will appreciate.

Watch a *sunset* together. Cheesy? Maybe. Romantic? Definitely.

Find out what their favorite toy was when they were younger and gift it to them. It's a sweet and *nostalgic* way to bring a smile to your partner's face.

Write them a *letter* and send it through the mail—even if you two live together. Watch the joy that cascades down their face when they open it.

If they've been having a rough week, give them the opportunity to *sleep in*. Slip out of bed and try to be as quiet as possible.

Don't cut them off when you're arguing. *Respect* them enough to let them say their piece, even in the heat of the moment.

Go on a spontaneous adventure together. The adventure itself is completely up to the two of you, and it can be as big or small as you choose. As long as it's spur-of-the-moment and gets your blood pumping, it's an *adventure*.

Do chores together. Let one another know that you're invested in maintaining your shared space. You can also play music while you work and come up with *creative* ways to make the tasks a game!

Create a new *recipe* together. It can be as involved or as simple as you'd like. Write it down and then put it together the next time you have a special occasion to celebrate.

Wake them up with a quickie. It's guaranteed to put a *smile* on their face for the rest of the day.

Indulge in *their* ***indulgences*** for once instead of teasing them about them. Buy their favorite perfume, pick up a book about something they are really interested in, or splurge on an expensive dinner.

Plan themed ***gift exchanges***. They can be as creative or as simple as you'd like. There's something about working within a certain theme that makes gift-giving extra special—and superfun too.

GO WITH THEM TO IMPORTANT APPOINTMENTS—WHETHER IT'S A REGULAR CHECKUP, AN ACUPUNCTURIST, OR A FERTILITY SPECIALIST. EVEN IF YOU CAN'T GO INTO THE ACTUAL APPOINTMENT, JUST KNOWING THAT YOU'RE IN THE WAITING ROOM WILL MAKE YOUR PARTNER FEEL *supported*.

Allow your partner a little *buffer* when they get home from work. Don't jump all over them—say hello and then give them a twenty-minute window to decompress alone. You may find that you enjoy that time to yourself too.

Compromise when it comes to how you spend your free time. If they like to have more time alone, but you want to spend more time as a couple, figure out a middle ground and schedule your time accordingly. Scheduling time together may not seem sexy, but it's a simple and important way to show that you're invested in your relationship and the happiness of both you and your partner.

Take care of things before a situation is dire. If something in the relationship has been bothering you, or you feel budding negativity toward your partner, **don't wait** for the "perfect" time to bring it up. There is never a *good* time to talk about something troublesome: whether you are having a great day or a terrible day, problems are not fun. If you wait and wait to bring it up, your emotions—and the problem—will continue to grow, causing more issues when things finally spill over.

Keep healthy food in the house for the both of you. It may not be as sexy as a massage, but investing in their **wellness**—and yours—shows your partner that you plan for the two of you to be together for a long time.

Make sure your hellos and goodbyes are special. This doesn't even necessarily mean that you kiss them every time. You can high-five, tousle their hair, or give them a **little pinch** on the bum if they're into that.

Send them *funny GIFs* or pictures throughout the day. Nothing says "I'm thinking of you" quite like a sassy meme.

Tell them how good they make you feel in bed—and *be specific*. Even if you're not into dirty talk, it's an easy way to let your partner know that they're satisfying you sexually.

Don't bring up past disappointments in a *current* fight.

TAKE CARE OF YOUR OWN ***mental health***. THIS COULD MEAN TRYING A MEDITATION PRACTICE OR FINALLY GETTING YOURSELF INTO THERAPY. BEING ABLE TO KEEP YOURSELF HEALTHY MENTALLY MEANS THAT YOUR PARTNER DOESN'T ALWAYS END UP SHOULDERING THAT BURDEN, AND THAT IS A GIFT TO BOTH THEM *AND* YOU.

Don't condescend. It is the absolute least loving (and least effective) way to ***communicate*** with your partner.

Surprise them with a ***lavish*** gift. Pinch your pennies and splurge for a big occasion—or just because. Money doesn't buy happiness, of course, but spoiling your partner from time to time is a sweet way of showing them just how special they are.

Plan a ***romantic getaway*** for their birthday. Indulge in all the couple-centric things that location has to offer.

Have a day where you allow them to decide everything you do, then *switch roles* the following day. It's a fun way to ensure that you're both spending time the way you want to. Plus, you may find out something about your partner that surprises you.

Ask them about the things that turn them on in the *bedroom*. What do you do that they love? What do they want more of? Direct questions are a fast and easy way to clear up any confusion and improve your skills in the bedroom.

PLAY WITH THEIR HAIR. IT'S INCREDIBLE HOW *relaxing* THIS ONE SIMPLE ACT CAN BE.

Plan an entire date around something they love. If they're big pizza fans, take your own pizza tour of a city. If they're interested in museums, spend the day museum hopping. Not only does it show that you know and care about your partner's ***interests;*** it's also an easy way to demonstrate your desire to share with them too.

Surprise them with ***tickets*** to their favorite sporting event. Let them know that they can go with you *or* someone else—and be excited for whichever option they choose.

KEEP LITTLE TRINKETS AND SOUVENIRS—LIKE RECEIPTS, TICKET STUBS, OR POSTCARDS—FROM YOUR DATES OR TRIPS TOGETHER. COMPILE THEM ALL INTO A *scrapbook* AND GIVE IT TO YOUR PARTNER AS A GIFT.

Place a ***hand*** on their leg when you're sitting side by side.

Come up with a ***code word*** or phrase that means "I love you" without actually saying "I love you." Some people can be shy about declaring their love out loud, especially in the company of others. Code words allow you to express yourself while also showing respect for their comfort (or yours). Plus, it's super intimate—and fun—to share special code words with your partner.

TAKE A ***selfie***. IN FACT, TAKE AS MANY SELFIES AS NEEDED UNTIL YOU'RE BOTH HAPPY WITH THE RESULT.

Post a celebratory social media ***status*** about them. Sure, social media PDA can be a bit uncomfortable when done too often, but every once in a while it's a sweet way to show the world how much you care. And trust that it will make your partner smile and even blush.

Slip their ***favorite sweet*** into their purse or briefcase for them to find at work.

Get into the shower with them for a sweet and ***sudsy surprise***.

If they're into sexy undergarments, have them come ***shopping*** with you so they can pick out something they would like you to wear. Slip it on the next time you want to get frisky.

Play *footsie* under the table.
There's a reason this move is a classic.

If they have a specific hobby, learn the *lingo*. This way, you actually know what they're talking about when they recount golf matches or video game plays.

Let them know how *lucky* you feel to be with them.

Be a friend. Sure, when it comes to your relationship you always want to be a lover. True intimacy, however, comes when the person you're with is someone you turn to for romance *and* *friendship*.

Be the ***real*** you. A partner who truly loves you will never want you to put on a mask or stifle your wants or needs just to please them. The more comfortable you are with yourself around your partner, the closer the two of you will feel.

Let them know that you ***miss*** them when you're separated. Send them a selfie, shoot them an email, or just call them to say hello.

Make a ***gift certificate*** book for them filled with tasks you will do. Certificates can range from "make the bed" to "spend a night in" to "give me a kiss *immediately*." Get creative and have fun with it!

WRAP YOUR ARMS AROUND THEIR WAIST WHILE THEY'RE WASHING THE DISHES, DOING LAUNDRY, OR COOKING DINNER. ***Physical displays*** OF LOVE SHOW YOUR PARTNER THAT YOU APPRECIATE THEIR WORK. PLUS, IT HELPS MAKE A CHORE FEEL LESS LIKE A CHORE.

When going out, pick a table where you two can sit side by side. ***Snuggle*** close to one another. You might be surprised by how much intimacy this one simple trick can cultivate.

Stick a ***love note*** on their laptop keyboard for them to see the next time they open it.

GIVE THEM A QUICK ***kiss*** IN PUBLIC.

Create a *relationship playlist* with songs that make you think of each other. Play it when you're apart or when you're having an argument. It will remind you both why you love one another.

The next time you're on a road trip, pull the car over and indulge in a sexy, impromptu *make-out* session. Spontaneity keeps things spicy.

Try to read between the lines when they're talking to you. It can be difficult, but you might uncover deeper meaning in what they are saying or asking. For example, if your partner keeps talking about a romantic trip that a coworker took, it might be a *hint* that they'd like to take an intimate vacation with you in the near future.

IF THEY CHANGE THEIR HAIR, TAKE NOTICE AND *compliment* THEM!

Let them enjoy time away from you without checking in constantly. There's a *fine line* between letting your partner know you're thinking of them and being a pest.

Bring up issues *directly* with them, as tempting as it may be to just complain to a close confidante. Talking behind your partner's back cultivates negativity and affects the way those close friends or family members view your partner—especially if all they hear about are the annoyances or arguments.

Do the *food shopping* together. It shows that you'll use any excuse to spend time with one another and has the added benefit of ensuring you both end up with food you love.

If they like a certain brand of gum or mints, keep a pack ***on hand*** for them to enjoy. They'll be especially grateful after that onion bagel!

Sneak up behind them and give them a kiss when they're distracted by their phone or laptop. Remember, loving gestures don't always have to be over the top. Love is cultivated in the little moments too.

Acknowledge ***Valentine's Day*** even if you think it's cheesy. It's an excuse to celebrate your love for one another—and who doesn't want that?

Have an event coming up that calls for a costume? Pick a ***couple's costume***. Get elaborate with it too: try a throwback, like Sonny and Cher, using clothing you found at a thrift store, or opt for costumes that require a major hair or makeup moment, like zombies or eighteenth- century French nobility. Not only will it be a fun activity for you and your partner; you're sure to delight others as well.

If you play a musical instrument, write a ***song*** for them. Covers are also sweet, especially if the song means something to you both.

If they're coming down with a cold, pick up their cold medicine—and their favorite type of tea or *soup* while you're at it. Going to the store when you're sick is never fun, and your partner will appreciate the extra time to focus on getting better.

Dedicate a song to them. It can be on the radio, at a concert, or just in your living room.

Volunteer TOGETHER FOR A CAUSE THAT MEANS A LOT TO EITHER—OR BOTH—OF YOU.

Have a sober ***date night*** where you do something sweet or silly together. This could mean a round of mini golf, a trip to the local ice cream stand, or a long walk on the beach. Having the occasional booze-free date allows you and your partner to connect on levels that can be harder to reach when drinking. Plus, when a date isn't centered around alcohol, it gives you the opportunity to explore activities you may not have tried (or been able to try) otherwise, such as rock climbing and cooking.

If they want to have a serious conversation, take it seriously. Don't goof off or make a joke; truly take their concerns to ***heart*** and treat them with the respect they deserve.

When they say something is important to them, like a goal they've set for the coming year or a ***milestone*** they'd like to cross in the next month, help them make it happen. Whether you fuel their ambition with coffee and snacks or roll up your sleeves and help them get the job done, your devotion to their happiness is sure to make the difference.

Sing a ***karaoke duet*** together. Bonus points if it's a song that means something to the two of you.

If you're running late, let them know. It takes two seconds to send a ***text message***, and your partner will appreciate not being left hanging.

Go to an *amusement park* together.
Get cotton candy, try out all the rides, and win your partner a stuffed animal. It's a nostalgic way to add a bit of extra joy to your relationship.

Forgive AND MOVE ON. DON'T START THE SAME ARGUMENT OVER AND OVER AGAIN.

Protect them when you can, but let them *defend* themselves too.

Have an inside joke. You'll love the feeling of sharing a *laugh* whenever you think of it.

Refrain from *flirting* too much with others if it is uncomfortable for your partner. And if you always seem to find yourself in situations where others are flirting with you, figure out a way to politely remove yourself from those situations.

Re-create your *first date*. If the situation is not one that you can re-create (maybe the season is wrong or the restaurant isn't open anymore), get as close to the original date as you can.

SPEND A *cozy* SUNDAY INDOORS. STAY IN COMFY CLOTHES, CUDDLE A LOT, AND SPEND THE TIME DOING THINGS YOU TRULY LOVE TO DO TOGETHER AT HOME. IN FACT, YOU MAY DECIDE TO NEVER EVEN LEAVE THE BED...

Go for a *spontaneous* bike ride. Ride to a neighborhood that you've always wanted to explore, or just see where the day takes you. It's a mini adventure for the two of you—and you don't even have to go far.

Pick a show to watch or *podcast* to listen to together and stick with it. Don't do that one activity without the other person—even if it means you have to wait until they're around.

Ask them what makes them feel special. If it's something you can help with, then do so.

Splurge on a couple's ***spa day*** together.
Try a mud bath, hang out in the steam room together, and enjoy the time relaxing side by side. Being pampered yourself is great, but seeing your partner get pampered as well? That is both sweet *and* sexy.

Join a ***workout*** class together. Not only will it help keep you both accountable for staying (or getting) in shape, but it's also an easy way to squeeze in extra time together throughout the day.

Play in the ***snow*** together. Build a snowman, go sledding, or toss a few snowballs around. Playfulness is paramount in a relationship—so why not act like kids who are home from school for a snow day?

Go to the ballet or opera together. Hold one another's hands in the dark and enjoy the glamorous, captivating experience of being in a ***theater***. Afterward, you can go for a drink and discuss what you enjoyed about the show.

Do they like the way they look in a certain ***shirt*** you own but love too much to part with? Or find your favorite flannel to be so comfortable? Buy them the same piece that they can wear any time.

Have a ***bowling*** date. It's fun and pleasantly old-fashioned. Get a little competitive and place a wager on the outcome of the match. The winner has to cook dinner for a week.

Spend time with ***other couples***. Seeing how other couples interact can help you look at your own partnership from a different perspective. This isn't to say that you should compare your relationship to others, but witnessing a couple's sweet nicknames for one another or the way one pulls out the chair for the other might inspire you.

If you know there's an ***action*** that irritates your partner, avoid doing it. Don't burp in public if that's a pet peeve of theirs. Don't leave your wet towel on the bed if it makes their skin crawl. These acts might seem harmless to you, but they are little cuts that can eventually add up to a larger wound that kills your partnership.

Celebrate when they hit a specific ***goal***. Write them a card, bake them a cake, or just do a little happy dance for them.

Go bar hopping. Sure, fancy date nights are a blast, but sometimes you just want to clink beer cans, throw some darts, and split a plate of *pub nachos*. A low-key date night is the perfect way to remind yourselves that it's not about the money you spend on a date; it's about the time you spend with one another.

LEND THEM YOUR *coat* WHEN THEY'RE FEELING CHILLY. YES, EVEN IF THAT MEANS YOU'LL BE A BIT COLD.

Host a *game night* together. Teaming up with your partner to host a party will always bring the two of you together...but teaming up against your pals in an exciting game of charades? That's some serious relationship teamwork.

COMBINE *traditions*, ESPECIALLY ONES THAT NEITHER OF YOU WISHES TO COMPROMISE ON. THERE IS A MIDDLE GROUND FOR EVERYTHING, AND BY MESHING YOUR DIFFERENT CUSTOMS, YOU CAN CREATE BEAUTIFUL NEW ONES TOGETHER.

Let them take the reins from time to time. If you're usually the one to organize what you do on vacations, and they want to plan something, let them do it without micromanaging. Just ***sit back*** and enjoy the day off!

Have a lovemaking session where you're completely focused on their ***needs***. Your partner's pleasure should be just as important as yours, and spending an entire sexual encounter 100 percent focused on them shows that you understand and care about that.

Slip into something sexier than your typical pajama set one night before bed. Things are about to get ***steamy***...

Wander around a ***flea market***. Even better, set a small dollar amount and see how creative you can get in finding fun trinkets for each other that don't exceed that budget.

Instead of a dinner date, have a ***breakfast date***. Go to a diner and order a big stack of pancakes to share, or whip up something at home, setting the table as you would for a fancy dinner. Pull out a crisp tablecloth, light some candles, and look into one another's eyes as you enjoy your bacon.

Indulge in seasonally appropriate activities, like apple picking, pumpkin carving, or going for a sleigh ride. The ***holidays*** can be a whirlwind of obligations and stress, so taking some time to appreciate the season with your partner will remind you both what it's all about.

Make your favorite ***takeout*** food at home. Whether it's pepperoni pizza or sweet and sour pho, re-creating (or attempting to re-create) your favorite delivery staple together is a great way to bond *and* save a little cash. You may even find that you enjoy your version better.

Do some ***tourism*** in your own city together. Hop on a double-decker bus if one is available to you, or just take in the sights by foot. You may stumble upon a new favorite spot together.

Put together a surprise day with their closest ***friends***. Ask their pals to help you plan, and then get your partner to the surprise meet-up spot. It's up to them whether you tag along or not—but be excited for either outcome.

Keep certain aspects of your relationship in *confidence*. Don't go blabbing to your friends about everything that goes on between you two. It's important to vent, but having things that are just for the two of you will keep your relationship sacred.

If there's an event or a place they have to go to that you know they aren't looking forward to, *go with them.*

At the beginning of the year, write a list of goals you'd like to *achieve* together over the next 365 days. Hang it somewhere conspicuous, and then every time you complete a goal, check it off. At the end of the year, celebrate your accomplishments.

TELL THEM WHAT CAUGHT YOUR *eye* WHEN YOU FIRST MET THEM. NOSTALGIA IS INCREDIBLY ROMANTIC.

Slip a gift certificate into their wallet to their favorite *lunch spot*. They'll love the gesture as much as they'll love having lunch taken care of.

On small pieces of paper, write down the things that you love about one another. Put the pieces of paper in a jar. The next time you fight, pull out a couple of pieces from the jar and read them out loud. The easy *reminder* of your love will help defuse things that much faster.

Do they have a pet? Buy ***treats*** or a new fun toy for their companion! It's an easy way to show your partner that you care not only about them but also about the furry (or scaly or feathery) friend in their life.

Respect their ***boundaries***. If they hate birthdays, don't go and throw them a huge surprise party. If they've made it clear that they don't want a relationship with a parent, don't push the subject. Knowing which lines to toe shows that you are respectful of them and their comfort.

BE YOUR OWN PERSON.
HAVE HOBBIES AND FRIENDS THAT YOU ENJOY WITHOUT YOUR PARTNER. IT MAY SOUND COUNTERINTUITIVE, BUT HAVING A LIFE OUTSIDE OF YOUR PARTNER HIGHLIGHTS THE TRUST YOU HAVE FOR ONE ANOTHER AND REMINDS YOU BOTH OF WHAT MAKES THE OTHER *unique*.

Have a mini ***camping*** excursion in your backyard. It's not exactly roughing it, but it's a great way to enjoy the romantic aspects of camping, like sleeping under the stars, without dealing with the less-than-glamorous aspects, like not having indoor plumbing available when nature calls.

Avoid constantly seeking ***validation*** from your partner. Looking for the occasional compliment is fine, but the second you rely on your partner as your go-to source for confidence, you suck the romance out of the relationship—and lose your ability to find confidence within yourself.

Don't make excuses when you've done something wrong. And work on avoiding those mistakes in the future—it's a good way to ***grow*** not only in your relationship but also as a person.

Complete a puzzle together. Working with your partner to figure out a ***puzzle*** is a great way to build your problem-solving *and* teamwork skills.

Go for a couple's ***massage***. It's a relaxing—and sexy—way for you to spend time together.

Have ***coffee*** together before work. You can do this at home or at a public spot you both enjoy. Taking some time for one another first thing in the morning sets the tone for the rest of your day.

If they have an online ***inspiration board*** or wish list where they save things they like, peruse it and pick them a gift from that board or list.

Always walk into and out of an event together. It's a subconscious way of showing the world that the two of you are *together*.

Adopt a ***pet*** together (just be sure you and your partner feel completely ready for it!). It's incredible how much love can grow between two people when they're caring for something together. Seeing how your partner interacts with a beloved dog or cat is sure to make your heart swell.

Grow something together, like a mini garden or a ***houseplant***. It doesn't matter if you both lack green thumbs. Just attempting to grow something is a sweet way to create a tangible display of the nurturing you both give to your relationship.

VISIT A RELATIONSHIP *counselor*—EVEN IF YOUR RELATIONSHIP IS GOING WELL. IT CAN HELP TO UNCOVER POTENTIAL PROBLEM AREAS OR JUST LEARN MORE ABOUT THE INNER WORKINGS OF YOUR PARTNER.

Pick up their dry cleaning. No one ever wants to do this for themselves, so your partner will feel like they've won the *lottery* when they see you've taken care of it.

Help them pick out a gift for a friend or family member. Not everyone is a natural when it comes to giving *gifts*. Helping your partner pick out something special for someone shows that you care about their other relationships too.

Rest your hand on their lower back or loosely hold on to their arm when walking behind them through a door. It's a simple gesture that shows your *connection* to one another.

Put yourself in their shoes. Don't think about how *you* would feel in a certain situation: try to see things from *their* perspective. Nothing says "I love you" like "I get how you're feeling," so strive for true ***understanding***.

SEND THEM A LOVING ***email*** AT WORK. SNAIL MAIL MAY BE CLASSIC, BUT EMAIL CAN BE JUST AS ROMANTIC.

Tell them what you need in bed. It's common for people to be afraid of pointing a partner in the right direction for fear of upsetting them. However, talking ***honestly*** about sex, and having a pleasurable sex life, is an important part of a healthy relationship. Letting your partner know how to please you is the first step.

Bake a ***cake*** to celebrate a small milestone in your relationship. What's sweeter than a "first time we made love" cake?

Re-create a childhood ***memory*** with them. It could be a vacation they took or a meal their mother made on a special occasion.

Wash their car. Bonus points if they get to watch you do it—and you make it ***sexy***.

IF THEY'RE SPIRALING ABOUT A SITUATION THAT NEEDS TO BE HANDLED, TAKE IT OFF THEIR HANDS AND ENCOURAGE THEM TO DO SOMETHING FOR THEMSELVES. GIVE THEM THE *space* TO NAP, TAKE A LONG BATH, OR GO FOR A WALK WHILE YOU TACKLE THE TASK.

Never say "I told you so."
Seriously, it's the worst.

Warm up their car on a cold ***morning***.
They'll appreciate the gesture—and will revel in the opportunity to slip into an already-warm car when it's time to leave for work.

Whisper in their ear how sexy they look.

Bring them a cold (or hot) drink when they're doing a chore that benefits both of you. It shows your ***appreciation*** *and* ensures your partner is taking care of themselves.

If you're handy, *repair* a problem with their car, bathtub, kitchen sink—whatever needs fixing. It will save money and show that you care.

Don't expect them to read your mind. People are most often misunderstood when they are vague. Help your partner to understand your thoughts or *feelings* by telling them exactly what you're thinking.

Thank THEM FOR JUST BEING WHO THEY ARE.

Check in with them before you make plans. This doesn't mean you have to ask them for permission to hang out with your friends, but seeing if your partner has already thought about possible activities for the two of you that weekend, or was hoping for your help with a certain project that day, shows them that they are an important *factor* in your decisions.

If they cook dinner, do the **dishes** without being asked. It's a sweet way to show your appreciation and let your partner know that you consider this a partnership.

Learn to mix their favorite **cocktail**. Have it waiting for them when they get home from work. Watch their face explode into a huge smile, and prepare for many kisses as your "thank you."

Warm up their cold hands. Rub them together in your own hands or slip them into your jacket *pocket*.

Tell them you love them every time you feel it—not just on *special occasions*. It's incredible how easy it is to forget to let your loved ones know how you feel about them, especially when, to you, those feelings seem obvious. Make sure to tell your partner often.

Give as much as you take. There are always going to be times when one partner needs more than the other and vice versa; however, if one partner is constantly taking while the other is constantly giving, it creates an imbalance that can lead to resentment. *Balancing* give with take keeps any one partner from becoming fatigued and helps you both trust that the other will be there when you need them.

LET THEM HAVE THE LAST BITE OF *dessert*. WHAT'S MORE LOVING THAN THAT?

Ask them about something that's on their ***bucket list***, then accomplish it together. It can be small—like trying a new cuisine, or big—like traveling to an exotic location.

Iron their shirt or suit the night before a big meeting or presentation at work. It's one less thing they have to worry about.

Buy their favorite snack and stash it in their car or work bag for them to find later. Not only will it give them a nice ***energy boost***; it's an easy way to show that you thought of them.

Carpool together when possible. Not only is it environmentally friendly; it's also a good excuse to spend some more time together at the beginning and end of the day.

Learn to love yourself. The old adage is true: it *is* difficult to love others when you don't love yourself. Putting in the work to build that **self-love** is an important act of personal care and ensures that you're bringing your best self to your relationship with your partner.

Give them time to spend with their family without you. It's easy to expect that you'll be invited to just about everything your partner is invited to, but sometimes it's nice to let them connect with the people in their lives **one-on-one**. Give them the space to nurture these other relationships.

Ask them questions when they speak. It shows them that you're ***invested*** in what they have to say, and that is a great gift.

Share your ***wildest dreams***. The crazier the better! It takes a great leap of faith to let someone in on the aspirations you've mostly kept to yourself. Opening up in this way shows immense trust in your partner.

Make a piece of ***art*** for them. It doesn't have to be big, involved, or even particularly good. Sometimes people are better at expressing themselves through mediums such as sculpture or painting than they are through conversation. So, if you want to let your partner know what they mean to you, and are at a loss for words, get a little crafty.

Go on a couple's *retreat*. It doesn't necessarily have to be focused on improving relationships, either. Any situation that gives you the opportunity to be together and focus on your relationship counts.

Follow through on your ***promises***. It's the simplest way to build trust in a relationship.

Be respectful of their time. Don't make plans for them without consulting them first. Don't assume that they'll always be around. Your partner has a life outside of you, and it is important to ***respect*** that.

SAY *thank you* WITH A KISS, HUG, OR SMILE INSTEAD OF WORDS. ACTIONS SPEAK LOUDER, AFTER ALL.

Take the *Love Language* test with your partner, then tailor your affection to their results (and vice versa).

Do simple tasks for them, like picking up their *laundry* or putting on a pot of tea, if they've been feeling under the weather.

Keep a framed picture of the two of you on your desk. It helps keep them at the front of your *mind* and tells them that you want to show them off.

TOO COLD FOR AN *outdoor picnic*? PLAN A CUTE ONE ON THE FLOOR OF YOUR APARTMENT.

Thank them when they make you feel special. Even if it's a tiny act, ***acknowledging*** how they make you feel instantly binds you two together—and lets your partner know what to do more of in the future.

Participate in some healthy competition. Race each other on your bikes, play a ***board game***, or challenge each other with some pickup basketball. The winner gets a foot massage from the loser, naturally.

Teach them how to love you. Sometimes people don't know the best ways to show their love, and what one partner needs can be different from what another partner needs. Tell your partner how they can best love *you*. This could be just letting them know that you aren't into PDA, or telling them how to help you calm down after an anxiety attack. A good partner will also be a good student when the subject in question is you.

Avoid always needing to have the last word. It's more important to be ***kind*** than it is to be right...in relationships *and* in life.

If you're leaving and they're still asleep, give them a kiss before you head out. They're unlikely to mind being roused by something as ***sweet*** as a kiss before you sneak out the door.

Do their laundry. Especially if it's a chore they hate while you don't mind it. It's a simple way to bring a little more *pleasure* to their day.

If you borrow their car, make sure to return it in the condition you found it. Don't leave trash in the back seat, or the gas gauge on empty. Respecting your partner's property shows them that you *respect* them too.

Dress alike from time to time. This doesn't mean you have to full-on twin, but wearing matching or *coordinating colors* lets people know that the two of you are together. Plus, it's fun!

Pick a week where you do something extra kind for them every day. Leave a piece of *chocolate* on their pillow or pick up their favorite coffee beverage and bring it to their work. One little act each day can do wonders for your relationship.

Like their *social media* posts. It may seem silly, but it's a quick and easy way to let them know that you're interested in the goings-on of their day.

Touch them and make eye contact at the same time. One action *affirms* the other. Throw in an "I love you" as well, and you'll be golden.

If you both like to cook, compile all of your shared favorite recipes into a handmade ***cookbook*** and gift it to them. Not only is it a darling little keepsake; it's also incredibly practical.

Invite them along on a ***business trip*** if you're able. It will be a nice break for them *and* for you. There's nothing better than coming back to a hotel room and seeing your partner waiting there for you.

Turn to them first. If you're having an issue, make them the person you call or the ***shoulder*** you cry on.

HELP THEM TO SEE THE POSITIVE SIDE OF A SITUATION. YOU DON'T HAVE TO ALWAYS BE AN *optimist*, BUT SOMETIMES PEOPLE NEED SOMEONE TO SHOW THEM THE GOOD THINGS WHEN THEY ARE UNABLE TO SEE THEM FOR THEMSELVES. BE THAT PERSON FOR YOUR PARTNER.

Ask their parent to teach you how to cook their favorite meal—then *surprise* them with it.

Focus on the *positives* in your relationship rather than the negatives. Don't sweep arguments and disagreements under the rug, but make an effort to always note the good things (you can make a list if that helps), especially with a situation that feels desperate.

Be *responsible*. It's easy to assume that a good relationship is just going to carry on swimmingly, doing its own thing. However, it takes constant maintenance for it to remain strong. Take ownership of your relationship and work at it together.

Point out things that they may enjoy. If they love dogs, make sure they don't miss the *adorable* puppy in the window you are about to walk past.

Slow down and take pleasure in those seemingly mundane parts of your life together. "Boring" is a state of mind. Find ways to appreciate, even celebrate, the minute aspects of your partnership: they tend to be the things you miss most when they're gone.

If they're in a rush, check the traffic and let them know the best route to take. It's a *small gesture* that can change their entire day for the better.

If they're going to be coming home late, leave them a plate of *dinner* ready to be warmed up. No one likes to go to bed hungry, and having something already prepared will make your partner incredibly happy. Just make sure to leave them a note so they know it's in the refrigerator!

Leave a voice mail message when you know they will be away from their phone. Text messages are sweet, but hearing your partner's *voice* saying "I love you" is enough to make any heart sing. Your partner can save the message, too, and listen to it whenever they want.

CREATE A *change jar* THAT YOU BOTH CONTRIBUTE TO. ONCE THE CHANGE REACHES A CERTAIN AMOUNT, SPEND IT ON SOMETHING SPECIAL LIKE A DINNER—DO *NOT* SPEND IT ON BILLS!

Learn to comfortably share a *silence*.
Sit together, hold hands, read a book, and don't speak.
This is true intimacy.

Take in a comedy show. Nothing bonds people like *laughter*.

Rent their favorite *movie* and spend the evening on the couch. Pop some popcorn, stock up on some good candy, and cuddle.

Write them a thank-you note. It can be a paper note or an email, but the physicality of the "thank you" gives it a little something *special*.

Talk out jealous feelings. Whether it's from them showing attention to another person or crossing a professional milestone, jealousy can be a huge obstacle in a relationship. Although it is not easy to admit when you are jealous, don't bottle up that emotion so it eventually overflows. *Communicate* feelings of jealousy to your partner so you can work as a team to pinpoint the underlying cause and work to eradicate it.

One night a week, go to bed half an hour earlier than usual. Spend the extra time before you fall asleep cuddling and chatting. When life gets busy, it's easy to just collapse onto your bed late at night and immediately fall asleep. Building in that extra time with your partner ensures intimacy on even the craziest days—an easy way to help keep the *spark* alive in your relationship.

Remind them of upcoming birthdays, graduations, and other *special events*. Some people have trouble remembering it all—and not for lack of caring. Make it easier on them with a simple, "By the way, Father's Day is this Sunday."

Before you vent to them, ask if they have the emotional energy to handle it. Everyone wants their partner to help them through hard times, but taking on someone else's emotional load can be exhausting after a while. Asking if they are in the right *mental space* to listen and offer support shows that you respect their boundaries.

TRY A SEXY BOARD OR DICE GAME. *Games AND* INTIMACY—WHAT COULD BE MORE FUN?

Give them suggestions without parenting them. No one wants to be mothered by the person they're sleeping with. If they spend a lot of money on a luxury item, and you feel it may inhibit their ability to pay for something important later, explain your perspective on the situation and then ask for theirs. Lecturing is a one-way "conversation," so this ***equal*** back-and-forth keeps your partner from feeling patronized.

Don't take the air out of their balloon. If they say they want to do something that seems far-fetched, don't roll your eyes or point out the flaws in their vision. Let them ***dream***.

GIVE THEM CONTROL OF THE TV REMOTE FOR THE EVENING—ESPECIALLY IF YOU TEND TO HOG IT. THIS IS THE *ultimate gift* YOU CAN GIVE TO A PERPETUAL CHANNEL SURFER.

Introduce them to the important people in your life. It can be tempting to keep your partner and the rest of your life separate for fear of ruining your *love story* with the complexities of the "real world." However, introducing your partner to those who are meaningful to you shows that you want them to be a part of every aspect of your life.

If they're not going to be around to watch a sports game or an upcoming episode of their favorite show live, *record* it for them. It shows that you're tuned into what makes them happy.

Keep photos of the two of you in your shared space. It may seem small, but seeing photos of you as a couple helps remind both of you of the bond you share. The photos don't have to be professional or overly staged, either. Simple snapshots keep special *memories* alive and at the front of your minds.

If you have children together, share what you love about your partner with them. It's flattering to your partner, and sets a loving *example*.

Take a *personal day* from work together. See a movie, have a long lunch at your favorite restaurant, or just spend the day lounging around the house. Doing something that feels a little naughty together, like skipping work, is seriously fun. Plus, you'll be able to enjoy certain activities more because you won't be dealing with the usual weekend crowds.

The next time you're at a baseball game or other public event where the opportunity presents itself, splurge to have an "I love you" message displayed on the marquee. It's fun, a little cheesy, and guaranteed to make your partner *smile*.

If they're going to be coming home late from a trip or event, ***stay up*** to wait for them. No one likes to come back to a dark, quiet home, so greet them warmly when they come through the door. It will make their return that much sweeter.

Go puddle-jumping! Make the most of a rainy day together, *and* relish the chance to embrace your ***silly*** side. It is a simple activity that will become a favorite shared memory of how much you enjoy each other's company, even on those gloomy days.

Let them "steal" bites of your restaurant order. Yes, they could have ordered their own instead of saying they were fine, but ***sharing*** is sweet—and maybe your partner wanted a few French fries instead of *all* of them.

Say "please" and "thank you." It's a ***courtesy*** that you extend to waitstaff, bank tellers, and strangers who hold the door open, so why wouldn't you also extend it to your partner? Yes, they know you are not intending to be bossy and that you are thankful for what they do, but it is important to still say the words out loud.

Play a ***prank***. Seriously! Don't do anything damaging or that you know your partner isn't a fan of, but do get creative. It is exciting, unexpected, and will remind your partner of the fun you two have had together.

When your partner is away from their computer, tablet, or phone, change the screen saver to a photo collage of the two of you. It will be a ***sweet surprise***.

Talk about what things outside of your relationship make you feel insecure. You never know how things may also carry over into how you behave with your partner. Plus, being *vulnerable* shows trust, and trust is the foundation of a strong relationship.

Don't guilt them. No matter the *circumstances*, there is never a good reason for guilting your partner.

Ask them about even the smallest parts of their lives. Their favorite cereal can be just as *telling* as their college major.

Take a cheesy *photo booth* picture together. Keep it somewhere you'll see it often, like on your desk at work, or use it as a bookmark in the book you're reading.

PICK A RANDOM DAY TO DO SOMETHING FUN, AND THEN *repeat* IT ON THE SAME DAY EVERY YEAR. YOU'LL ALWAYS LOOK FORWARD TO APRIL 24 AS THE DAY YOU GET FALAFEL AND PEOPLE-WATCH IN THE PARK.

If the weather is going to be bad, arrange to drop them off or pick them up at work. It shows you care about them getting to their destination *safely*, even if you have to drive a bit out of your way.

Before they leave for a trip, spritz one of your shirts with your *perfume* or cologne and pack it in their suitcase. They'll have something to remind them of you the entire trip.

If they live far away from family, buy them a plane ticket. An opportunity to see *loved ones* they have been missing is more valuable than a piece of expensive jewelry or clothing could ever be.

Collaborate on a side hustle together. Whether it's cowriting a children's book, starting a true crime podcast, or working on a short film together, flexing your ambitious muscles side by side will open up an entirely new side of your relationship. Plus, if one of you isn't enjoying your full-time gig, working on this side venture together shows that the other is invested in helping their partner find something they are passionate about.

Let them take care of you. It can be uncomfortable to feel less than perfect with your partner, but admitting when you may need ***help*** (or just a cup of tea and a hug) and allowing them to care for you shows that you trust them.

If they're in a bad mood, play their favorite music or put on their favorite movie. Grab them by the hand and dance around or act out a scene of the film dramatically. Watch their *spirits* lift.

Warm up their towel in the dryer while they're showering so they can enjoy a little *luxury* when they step out of the stream. No dryer in your living space? Using a blow dryer works just as well.

Remember that it's sometimes important for you to put your own feelings aside and help your partner out from time to time. You may be absolutely done with the day and ready to curl up in a ball until the weekend, but going for a walk with them when they're feeling down can do more to boost their *mood* than going alone ever could.

Make "I love you" the first thing you tell them every morning and the last thing you tell them *every night.*

ABOUT THE AUTHOR

Maria Del Russo is a writer who regularly covers sex, relationships, and wellness. She is a regular contributor for *Playboy*. Her work has also been featured in *The Cut*, *The Washington Post*, *Glamour*, *InStyle*, *Refinery29*, *Coveteur*, and other outlets. She lives in Brooklyn. You can follower her on *Instagram* at @mariadelrusso and on *Twitter* at @maria_delrusso.